goRussian

Speak & Read the Pimsleur Way

· Reading Program ·

SIMON & SCHUSTER'S
PIMSLEUR

Hear it, Learn it, Speak it, Read it

For more information, call
1-800-831-5497 or visit us
at www.Pimsleur.com

Graphic Design: Maia Kennedy

© 2001-2009 Simon & Schuster, Inc. All Rights Reserved.
Pimsleur® is an imprint of Simon & Schuster Audio,
a division of Simon & Schuster, Inc.

PIMSLEUR® is a registered trademark of Beverly Pimsleur,
used by Simon & Schuster under exclusive license.
Graduated Interval Recall™ and Principle of Anticipation™ are trademarks of S&S.

goRussian

ACKNOWLEDGMENTS

VOICES
English-Speaking Instructor .... Ray Brown
Female Russian Speaker .... Lena Burtseva
Male Russian Speaker (I) .... Rustem Safranov
Male Russian Speaker (II) .... Andry Kagalovsky
Male Russian Speaker (III) .... Dmitry Kukunov

WRITERS
Christopher J. Gainty
Sergei Poletayev (I) • Nadja Berkovitch (II & III)

EDITORS
Dr. Ulrike S. Rettig
Mary E. Green • Beverly D. Heinle

GoRUSSIAN REVIEWERS
Larysa Smirnova • Masako D'Auria

EXECUTIVE PRODUCER
Beverly D. Heinle

PRODUCER & DIRECTOR
Sarah H. McInnis

RECORDING ENGINEERS
Peter S. Turpin • Kelly Saux

Simon & Schuster Studios, Concord, MA

goRussian

TABLE OF CONTENTS

User's Guide 1

Introduction 15

Cyrillic Alphabet 23

Part One 27

Part Two 63

Part Three 95

Pimsleur User's Guide   *go*Russian

Introduction

You have just purchased the most effective language program ever developed. As you probably know, learning a new language can be frustrating. Your first experience with a foreign language may have been in school. If the classes seemed difficult, or if your grades were poor, you probably believed you had no aptitude for languages. Even if you did well, you may have been surprised later to discover that what you learned was of little or no use when you tried to converse with native speakers.

Perhaps you waited until later in life and tried adult education classes, language schools, or home training programs. There too you may have found the information hard to retain, the lessons tedious, and your progress slow. Many language students give up early in these programs, convinced they lack the natural ability to understand and use what they read and hear.

The truth is that anyone can acquire a foreign language — with the right teaching system. With the Pimsleur® Method, you will benefit from the years of research and development that have helped create the world's most effective method for teaching foreign languages. The Pimsleur® Language Programs, developed by Dr. Paul Pimsleur, fill an urgent need for self-instructional materials in many languages.

Pimsleur User's Guide — *go*Russian

How to Use the Program

To get the full benefit of each lesson, choose a quiet place where you can practice without interruption and a time of day when your mind is most alert and your body least fatigued.

The length of each lesson, just under 30 minutes, is that recommended by teaching specialists for a concentrated learning task. Once you've started the program, simply follow the tutor's instructions. The most important instruction is to respond aloud when the tutor tells you to do so. There will be a pause after this instruction, giving you time to reply. It is essential to your progress that you speak out in a normal conversational voice when asked to respond. Your active participation in thinking and speaking is required for your success in mastering this course.

The simple test for mastery is whether you are able to respond quickly and accurately when your tutor asks a question. If you are responding correctly about eighty percent of the time, then you're ready to proceed to the next lesson. It is important to keep moving forward, and also not to set unreasonable standards of perfection that will keep you from progressing, which is why we recommend using the eighty percent figure as a guide.

Pimsleur User's Guide   *go*Russian

How to Use the Program (continued)

You will notice that each lesson contains both new and familiar material, and just when you may be worrying about forgetting something, you will conveniently be reminded of it. Another helpful feature of the Pimsleur® Language Program is its rate of "saturation." You will be responding many times in the half-hour. This saturation enables you to make substantial progress within a short period of time.

Guidelines for Success

Complete the lesson units in strict consecutive order (don't skip around), doing no more than one lesson per day, although the lesson unit for the day may be repeated more than once. Daily contact with the language is critical to successful learning.

Listen carefully to each lesson unit. Always follow the directions of the tutor.

Speak out loud when directed by the tutor and answer questions within the pauses provided. It is not enough to just silently "think" of the answer to the question asked. You need to speak the answer out loud to set up a "circuit" of the language you are learning to speak so that it is heard and identified through your ears, to help to establish the "sounds"

Pimsleur User's Guide — *go*Russian

Guidelines for Success (continued)

of the target language. Do this prior to hearing the confirmation, which is provided as reinforcement, as well as additional speech training.

Do all required activities according to the instructions, without reference to any outside persons, textbooks, or courses.

Do not have a paper and pen nearby during the lessons, and do not refer to dictionaries or other textbooks while doing the spoken lessons. The Pimsleur® Method works with the language-learning portion of your brain, requiring language to be processed in its spoken form. Not only will you interrupt the learning process if you attempt to write the words that you hear before learning to read in the new language, but you will also begin to speak the target language with an American accent. This is because the sounds represented by the American letters are frequently different from the sounds of the same-looking letters in the foreign language.

Pimsleur User's Guide — goRussian

Dr. Paul Pimsleur

Dr. Paul Pimsleur devoted his life to language teaching and testing and was one of the world's leading experts in applied linguistics. He was fluent in French, good in German, and had a working knowledge of Italian, Russian, Modern Greek, and Mandarin Chinese. After obtaining his Ph.D. in French and a Masters in Psychology from Columbia University, he taught French Phonetics and Linguistics at UCLA. He later became Professor of Romance Languages and Language Education, and Director of The Listening Center (a state-wide language lab) at Ohio State University; Professor of Education and Romance Languages at the State University of New York at Albany; and a Fulbright lecturer at the University of Heidelberg.

Dr. Pimsleur was a founding member of the American Council on the Teaching of Foreign Languages (ACTFL). His many books and articles revolutionized theories of language learning and teaching. After years of experience and research, Dr. Pimsleur developed a new method (The Pimsleur® Method) that is based on two key principles: the *Principle of Anticipation*™ and a scientific principle of memory training that he called *Graduated Interval Recall*™. This Method has been applied to the many levels and languages of the Pimsleur® Programs.

Pimsleur User's Guide *go*Russian

Graduated Interval Recall™

Graduated Interval Recall™ is a complex name for a very simple theory about memory. No aspect of learning a foreign language is more important than memory, yet before Dr. Pimsleur, no one had explored more effective ways for building language memory.

In his research, Dr. Pimsleur discovered how long students remembered new information and at what intervals they needed to be reminded of it. If reminded too soon or too late, they failed to retain the information. This discovery enabled him to create a schedule of exactly when and how the information should be reintroduced.

Suppose you have learned a new word. You tell yourself to remember it. However, after five minutes you're unable to recall it. If you'd been reminded of it after five seconds, you probably would have remembered it for maybe a minute, at which time you would have needed another reminder. Each time you are reminded, you remember the word longer than you did the time before. The intervals between reminders become longer and longer, until you eventually remember the word without being reminded at all.

This program is carefully designed to remind you of new information at the exact intervals where maximum retention takes place. Each time your memory begins to fade, you will be asked to recall the word.

Pimsleur User's Guide goRussian

Principle of Anticipation™

The *Principle of Anticipation*™ requires you to anticipate a correct answer. Practically, what this means is that you must retrieve the answer from what you have learned earlier in the course. It works by posing a question, asking you to provide a new sentence, using information you've learned previously and putting it into a new combination. This provides novelty and excitement which accelerates learning.

A possible scenario:

Speaker's cue: "Are you going to the movies today?"
--- PAUSE ---
Drawing on information given previously, you respond *(in the target language)*: "No, I'm going tomorrow."
The instructor will then confirm your answer:
"No, I'm going tomorrow."
The Narrator then may cue:
"Is your sister going to Europe this year?"
--- PAUSE ---
Response: "No, she went last year."

Before Dr. Pimsleur created his teaching method, language courses were based on the principle of "mindless-repetition." Teachers monotonously drummed words into the students' minds, as if there were grooves in the mind that could be worn deeper with repetition.

Pimsleur User's Guide — goRussian

Principle of Anticipation™ (continued)

Neurophysiologists tell us however, that on the contrary, simple and unchallenging repetition has a hypnotic, even dulling effect on the learning process. Eventually, the words being repeated will lose their meaning. Dr. Pimsleur discovered that learning accelerates when there is an "input/output" system of interaction, in which students receive information and then are asked to retrieve and use it.

Core Vocabulary

While *Graduated Interval Recall*™ and the *Principle of Anticipation*™ are the foundation of the Pimsleur® Method, there are other aspects that contribute to its uniqueness and effectiveness. One involves vocabulary. We have all been intimidated, when approaching a new language, by the sheer immensity of the number of new words we must learn. But extensive research has shown that we actually need a comparatively limited number of words to be able to communicate effectively in any language.

Language can be divided into two distinct categories: grammatical structures (function words) and concrete vocabulary (content words). By focusing on the former category and enabling the student to comprehend and employ the structure of the new

Pimsleur User's Guide — goRussian

Core Vocabulary (continued)

language, Dr. Pimsleur found that language learners were able to more readily put new knowledge to use. There are few content words that must be known and used every day. The essential "core" of a language involves function words, which tend to relate to human activities.

This course is designed to teach you to understand and to speak the essential elements of your new language in a relatively short time. During each half-hour lesson, you will actually converse with two native speakers, using the level of language spoken by educated citizens in their everyday business and social life. The program's unique method of presenting dialogue in-situation relieves you of the most common learning problem, the problem of meaning.

Organic Learning

The Pimsleur® Method centers on teaching functional mastery in understanding and speaking a language, in the most effective and efficient way possible. You will be working on your vocabulary, grammar, and pronunciation in an integrated manner, as you are learning specific phrases that have practical use in everyday activities.

Pimsleur User's Guide — *go*Russian

Organic Learning (continued)

There are several thousand languages in the world. Because fewer than five hundred of these languages have developed formal systems of writing, linguistic specialists accept that language is primarily speech. For this reason, it is also accepted that the human brain acquires language as speech. Therefore, when Dr. Pimsleur created his language programs, he began teaching with recorded materials, which enabled the learners to acquire the sounds, the rhythm, and the intonation of the target language. The learners did this more rapidly, more accurately, and with great enthusiasm because they found themselves capable of almost instant beginning communication skills.

Dr. Pimsleur called this "organic learning" because it involves learning on several fronts at the same time. His system enables the learner to acquire grammatical usage, vocabulary, and the sounds of the language in an integrated, exciting way. In short, the learner gains the language as a living, expressive form of human culture.

Pimsleur User's Guide — goRussian

"Reading" in a Pimsleur Program

A phonetic alphabet, such as the Latin alphabet and the Greek alphabet, is a list of symbols (letters) that are used to represent the sounds of the language in writing. And given that language is primarily speech, the spoken sounds of the language necessarily precede learning how to decode the written form, i.e., learning how to "read" – just as a child first learns to speak and then eventually to read. This is the natural progression Dr. Pimsleur followed in his courses.

After an initial introduction to the spoken language, reading is then integrated into the program and the new alphabet is systematically introduced, associating each letter with the sounds of the new language. Initially, you are sounding out words, mastering the different sounds associated with the new alphabet. You are not, at first, reading for meaning, but rather for sound/symbol correlation. Eventually, when the sound system is mastered, you will be able to look at known vocabulary and "read for meaning." By the end of the Comprehensive Level I course, you will be reading at the same level as you are speaking.

Course Content

When you have mastered a Pimsleur® Language Program, you will have a highly practical, everyday

Pimsleur User's Guide — goRussian

Course Content (continued)

vocabulary at your command. These basic words, phrases, and sentences have been carefully selected to be the most useful in everyday situations when you visit a foreign country. You will be able to handle social encounters graciously, converse with native speakers in travel situations, and use transportation systems with confidence. You'll be able to ask directions and to navigate your own way around the cities and countryside.

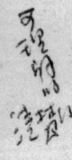

The language skills you learn will enable you to participate in casual conversations, express facts, give instructions, and describe current, past, and future activities. You will be able to deal with everyday survival topics and courtesy requirements. You will be intelligible to native speakers of the language — even to those who are not used to dealing with foreigners. What is equally important, you will know how to ask the kinds of questions that will further expand your knowledge of and facility with the language, because you will have been trained by the Pimsleur® open-ended questioning technique.

The Pimsleur® Method becomes a springboard for further learning and growth to take place — the ultimate purpose of any real educational system. This desire to learn will be apparent to the people with whom you speak. It will indicate sincere interest in and respect for their culture.

Pimsleur User's Guide   *go*Russian

A Note on Regional Language Differences

In any large country, and even in many smaller countries, regional differences in language are common. In the United States, for example, a person from Maine can sound very different than someone from Texas. Pronunciations ("accents") vary, and there are also minor differences in vocabulary. For example, what is called a "drinking fountain" in New York or Arizona is known as a "bubbler" in Wisconsin, and a "soft drink" in one part of America will be called a "soda" elsewhere. The differences in English are even more distinct between North Americans and Britons, or between Britons and Australians. But all are native speakers of English; all can communicate with spoken English, read the same newspapers, and watch the same television programs, essentially without difficulty.

Native speakers of a language can often tell where someone is from by listening to him or her speak. In addition to regional differences, there are social differences. Pimsleur® Language Programs use a standard "educated" speech, which will generally carry you throughout the country without difficulty.

goRussian

Speak & Read the Pimsleur Way

· Reading Program ·

INTRODUCTION

Introduction   goRussian
Pimsleur Reading Program

With *Pimsleur's Russian Reading Program*, you will learn to read Russian with the ease and flexibility of a native speaker. You will learn to sound out the Russian alphabet, starting with individual words, then word combinations and short phrases, increasingly building in length until you will be reading complete sentences in context. With practice, you will learn to read Russian fluidly for meaning, and you will be able to read it aloud with near-native pronunciation.

For maximum effectiveness, we recommend that you do the spoken lessons first, before starting the Reading Lessons. Hearing the spoken sounds first will help to introduce you to the new language.

There are three parts to this Reading Program. *Part One*, the sixteen Reading Lessons from *Pimsleur's Russian I, Third Ed.*, will introduce you to the Russian sound system.

Written Russian appears in the Cyrillic alphabet, the invention of which is traditionally credited to Saint Cyril, a ninth-century Russian monk. Today, the Cyrillic alphabet is also used to represent many

Introduction *go*Russian

Pimsleur Reading Program (continued)

of the (mainly Slavic) languages spoken in Eastern Europe, ranging from Belorussian to Macedonian. Derived from the Greek alphabet, Cyrillic is a phonetic system, with some symbols added or altered to represent sounds unique to these languages.

Since Russian is represented by the Cyrillic alphabet, you will need to learn to associate Russian sounds with what is probably a new system of symbols. If you are not familiar with the Cyrillic alphabet, you may at first find that it takes some time to associate the appropriate sounds with each letter and/or group of letters. Therefore, we recommend that you take the Reading Lessons at your own pace, repeating each until you feel comfortable proceeding with the next. With a little effort, you will be astonished at how quickly you are reading Russian.

A complete listing of the Cyrillic alphabet and the sounds of its letters follows, starting on page 23. You should use this for reference only, however, as all the information you need to do the readings is contained in the audio.

Introduction   *go*Russian

Pimsleur Reading Program (continued)

Although translations are provided, the meaning of the items at this point is secondary and we recommend you look at them only after first *reading* the sentences aloud, sounding them out with Russian pronunciation. The items have been selected especially to give you practice in the Russian sounds and sound combinations. Your vocabulary acquisition will begin after you've learned the new different sound system. You should read aloud, as directed. The process of saying the words out loud will reinforce acquisition and will help lodge the sounds in your memory. At this point you will be learning to read without an American accent.

Stress in Russian is variable and there is no universal rule as to the patterns of stress. Some guidelines are listed below:

• In Russian, almost every word is stressed. One-syllable particles are the main exception. Whether they are stressed or not depends on the surrounding words and the speaker, as well.

• Stress is an important part of correct pronunciation in Russian.

Introduction — goRussian

Pimsleur Reading Program (continued)

• Stress can change the sound of the vowels and even some of the consonants.

• Stress can be the only distinctive feature between words spelled identically. Typical examples of this are *muka* (torture/flour) and *slova* (genitive singular/nominative plural of *slovo*, "word").

• Stress marks are generally not used in written material. Textbooks and some dictionaries, however, put stress mark(s) on every word.

• Most nouns have regular, non-moving stress. On the other hand, many important nouns have shifting stress, which means that different forms of the same word may have the stress on different syllables.

• Long-form adjectives have regular stress, either on a root syllable, or at the end. In contrast, stress in short-form adjectives is flexible and different people will stress the same form differently.

• Verbs can also have shifting stress.

• Some fixed expressions have a stress of their own. An example is *ne bylo*, which is stressed on the *e* in *ne*, even though the word *bylo* is normally stressed on the *y*.

Pimsleur User's Guide   goRussian
Pimsleur Reading Program (continued)

Starting with Lesson 7, we have indicated where the stress is to be placed by showing the **stressed** vowel(s) in boldface.

Part Two contains fourteen Reading Lessons, the twelve Reading Lessons from *Pimsleur's Russian II, Second Ed.*, plus two additional lessons. This section will provide practice reading notes and selected Russian vocabulary for various topics such as the customs office, the subway, sightseeing, and the theater. You will continue to practice pronunciations of the Cyrillic letters and combinations of letters, as well as their use in different words and contexts. Translations are provided, but again, hold off on reading them until after you've read the words using your best Russian pronunciation. Remember to always speak aloud. Since you are working with a new sound system, you may wish to repeat some of the lessons. Repeat as you feel necessary. If you've completed Pimsleur's Russian II, most of the items will be familiar to you, and you'll be reading for meaning. If you haven't, then you will be learning new vocabulary, seeing and hearing it in context. We have

Pimsleur User's Guide — *go*Russian

Pimsleur Reading Program (continued)

again indicated where the stress is to be placed in the words by showing the **stressed** vowel(s) in boldface.

Part Three contains twenty more Reading Lessons, the Readings from *Pimsleur's Russian III, Second Ed.* In the first nine Lessons, you will continue to practice the pronunciation of the Cyrillic letters and combinations of letters. If you've completed *Pimsleur's Russian III*, most of the items in Lessons 10-20 will be familiar to you, allowing you to see how the known sounds and combinations of sounds are represented in print. If you haven't, then you will continue to be learning new vocabulary, seeing and hearing it in context. It's important that as you first read through each lesson, you concentrate on the recognition and pronunciation of the Cyrillic, regardless if the words are new or familiar. As before, we have indicated where the stress is to be placed in the words by showing the **stressed** vowel(s) in boldface. Again, all the lessons are accompanied by translation. We still recommend, however, that you do the Reading Lessons first, sounding them out carefully before you refer to the translations.

All instructions for doing the Readings are contained on the audio.

Cyrillic Chart

*go*Russian

Cyrillic Alphabet

The Cyrillic alphabet is comprised of 33 letters, listed in order below, along with a guide to the sounds represented by each letter. Many Russian letters (mostly vowels, but also some consonants) have more than one sound, depending on the amount of stress given to the letter or its position in the word. The examples listed in the "Guide to Pronunciation" are *approximate* English equivalents — as in any language, the pronunciations will vary slightly in different letter combinations.

Cyrillic letter (capital / small)	Guide to Pronunciation
А а	**a** as in *father* (when stressed); **u(h)** as in *mumps* (when unstressed)
Б б	**b** as in *bet* **p** at the end of a word
В в	**v** as in *vandal* **f** at the end of a word
Г г	**g** as in *gasoline* **k** at the end of the word sometimes **v** when in "г-о" combination
Д д	**d** as in *deep* **t** at the end of a word

Cyrillic Chart   goRussian

Cyrillic Alphabet *(continued)*

Cyrillic letter *(capital / small)*	Guide to Pronunciation
Е е	**ye** as in *yesterday* (when stressed); sometimes **e** as in *me* (when unstressed)
Ё ё	**yo** as in *yore*
Ж ж	**zh** as in the middle of the word *treasure*
З з	**z** as in *zoo* **s** at end of word
И и	**e** as in *eagle* (when stressed); **i** as in *big* or **e** as in *beg* (when unstressed)
Й й	the **y** at the end of *grey*
К к	**k** as in *Kafka*
Л л	**l** as in *Lenin*
М м	**m** as in *Moscow*
Н н	**n** as in *next*
О о	**o** as in *blow*, but shorter (when stressed); **o** as in *ostrich* (when unstressed), sometimes **u(h)** (when unstressed at the end of a word)
П п	**p** as in *Peter*
Р р	rolled **r**

Cyrillic Chart   *goRussian*

Cyrillic Alphabet *(continued)*

Cyrillic letter *(capital / small)*	Guide to Pronunciation
С с	**s** as in *so*
Т т	**t** as in *top*
У у	**oo** as in *tool*
Ф ф	**f** as in *find*
Х х	aspirated **h** as in *hot*
Ц ц	**ts** combination, as in *pits*
Ч ч	**ch** combination, as in *cheese*
Ш ш	**sh** as in *shoe*
Щ щ	longer, softer **sh** sound
Ъ ъ	*hard sign* - occurs between a consonant and a vowel -- adds an **ee** sound
Ы ы	fast **euh-ee** combination
Ь ь	*soft sign* - indicates that preceding letter should be pronounced softly
Э э	**e(h)** in *mess*
Ю ю	fast **ee-ou** combination; like -**eau**- in *beauty*
Я я	**ya** in *Yalta*, (when stressed); **ih** in *it* (when unstressed)

*go*Russian

Speak & Read the Pimsleur Way

· Reading Program ·

PART ONE

Part One

goRussian

TABLE OF CONTENTS

• •

Reading Lessons

Lesson One (Урок Один) 31
Lesson Two (Урок Два) 33
Lesson Three (Урок Три) 35
Lesson Four (Урок Четыре) 37
Lesson Five (Урок Пять) 39
Lesson Six (Урок Шесть) 41
Lesson Seven (Урок Семь) 43
Lesson Eight (Урок Восемь) 45
Lesson Nine (Урок Девять) 47
Lesson Ten (Урок Десять) 49
Lesson Eleven (Урок Одиннадцать) 51
Lesson Twelve (Урок Двенадцать) 53
Lesson Thirteen (Урок Тринадцать) 55
Lesson Fourteen (Урок Четырнадцать) 57
Lesson Fifteen (Урок Пятнадцать) 59
Lesson Sixteen (Урок Шестнадцать) 61

Part One
Урок Один

1. ма́ма
2. там
3. мат
4. том
5. мот
6. а́том
7. ром
8. рот
9. мор
10. мото́р
11. лото́
12. ра́ма
13. Ла́ра
14. ма́ло
15. Алло́?
16. молоко́
17. о́коло
18. ко́ка-ко́ла
19. Кто?
20. ка́рта

Part One

Lesson One

1. mom
2. over there
3. floor mat
4. volume
5. spendthrift
6. atom
7. rum
8. mouth
9. pestilence
10. motor, engine
11. lotto
12. frame
13. Lara, female first name
14. little
15. Hello? (on the telephone)
16. the milk (nominative case)
17. near
18. Coca-Cola
19. Who?
20. map

Part One

Урок Два

1. орáтор
2. тéло
3. лéто
4. мóре
5. мéра
6. мéтр
7. лет
8. я
9. ямá
10. моя́
11. моя́ мáма
12. éла
13. Я éла.
14. дом
15. Лáда
16. какáя
17. лéтом
18. дéло
19. Я дéлал.
20. Я дéлал дéло.

Part One
Lesson Two

1. orator
2. body
3. summer
4. sea
5. measure
6. meter
7. years (genitive case, plural)
8. I
9. hole, pit
10. my (feminine)
11. my mom
12. [I/She] was eating (feminine)
13. I was eating. (feminine)
14. house
15. Lada, female first name
16. which; how (feminine)
17. in the summer / in the summertime
18. business, work
19. I was doing. (masculine)
20. I was doing (masculine) work.

Part One
Урок Три

1. терем
2. драма
3. яд
4. вода
5. воля
6. сова
7. Вот сова.
8. Вот водка.
9. мир
10. лира
11. роса
12. слива
13. сидел
14. видел
15. Я видел.
16. Я вас видел.
17. далеко
18. в России
19. скоро
20. сестра

*go*Russian

Part One

goRussian

Lesson Three

1. tower
2. drama
3. poison
4. water
5. will; wishes
6. owl
7. Here's an owl.
8. Here's the vodka.
9. peace; world
10. lyre
11. dew
12. plum / plum tree
13. was sitting (masculine)
14. saw (masculine)
15. I saw. (masculine)
16. I saw (masculine) you.
17. far
18. in Russia
19. soon
20. sister

Part One
Урок Четыре

1. трава
2. метла
3. мастер
4. весна
5. вино
6. с вином
7. ресторан
8. в ресторане
9. юла
10. в юле
11. делаю
12. Я делаю.
13. блин
14. балет
15. билет
16. билет на балет
17. бокал
18. бокал вина
19. рядом
20. историю

Part One

Lesson Four

1. grass
2. broom
3. master
4. spring
5. wine
6. with wine
7. restaurant
8. in a / the restaurant
9. spinning top
10. in a spinning top
11. [I] do; [I]'m doing
12. I do; I'm doing.
13. pancake
14. ballet
15. ticket
16. ticket for ballet
17. a wine glass
18. a glass of wine
19. next [to]
20. history (accusative case)

Part One
goRussian
Урок Пять

1. родина
2. люди
3. верблюд
4. утро
5. удар
6. улетаю
7. Я улетаю утром.
8. папа
9. дупло
10. понимаю
11. Я понимаю.
12. пакет
13. картина
14. на картине
15. город
16. в городе
17. книга
18. в книге
19. в субботу
20. друг

Part One

goRussian

Lesson Five

1. homeland
2. people
3. camel
4. morning
5. punch; kick
6. [I'm] flying away.
7. I'm flying away in the morning.
8. dad
9. hollow
10. [I] understand
11. I understand.
12. packet
13. picture
14. in the picture
15. city
16. in the city
17. book
18. in the book
19. on Saturday
20. [good] friend (male)

Part One
Урок Шесть

1. гитара
2. моя гитара
3. парус
4. по-русски
5. Я не говорю ---
6. Я не говорю по-русски.
7. вы
8. Вы говорите.
9. Вы говорите по-русски.
10. И вы понимаете.
11. слушаю
12. Я слушаю.
13. Я вас слушаю.
14. Но не понимаю.
15. книга о России
16. на столе
17. Книга была на столе.
18. квартира
19. красивая
20. У вас красивая квартира.

Part One

Lesson Six

1. guitar
2. my guitar
3. sail
4. in Russian; Russian style
5. I don't speak ---
6. I don't speak Russian.
7. you (polite / plural)
8. You speak.
9. You speak Russian.
10. And you understand.
11. [I'm] listening
12. I'm listening.
13. I'm listening to you.
14. But [I] don't understand.
15. a book about Russia
16. on the table
17. The book was on the table.
18. an apartment
19. beautiful (feminine)
20. You have a beautiful apartment.

Part One *go*Russian

Урок Семь

1. работа
2. дорого
3. слишком дорого
4. это
5. Это еда.
6. Это слишком дорого.
7. аэропорт
8. в аэропорт
9. Мы едем в аэропорт.
10. хлеб
11. Вы хотите.
12. Вы хотите хлеба?
13. хлеба / хлеб
14. шоколад
15. Вы любите шоколад.
16. мать
17. мат
18. пять
19. шесть
20. Пять или шесть?

Part One

Lesson Seven

1. work / job
2. expensive
3. too expensive
4. this
5. This is food.
6. This / It is too expensive.
7. airport
8. to the airport
9. We are going to the airport.
10. bread
11. You want.
12. Do you want some bread?
13. some bread / bread
14. chocolate
15. You like [love] chocolate.
16. mother
17. floor mat
18. five
19. six
20. Five or six?

Part One   **goRussian**
Урок Восемь

1. Мне нравится.
2. Мне нравится пиво.
3. Вы хотите вина?
4. хочу
5. Хочу вино.
6. ты
7. четыре
8. тысяча
9. черепаха
10. знаете
11. Вы знаете.
12. здесь
13. здоровье
14. Я не знаю.
15. зубы
16. большой
17. Большой театр
18. новый
19. Новый год
20. С Новым годом!

Part One
Lesson Eight

1. I like [it].
2. I like beer.
3. Do you want some wine?
4. [I] want
5. [I] want the wine.
6. you [informal]
7. four
8. one thousand
9. turtle
10. [you] know
11. You know.
12. here
13. health
14. I don't know.
15. teeth
16. big
17. Bolshoi Theater
18. new
19. New Year
20. Happy New Year!

Part One
goRussian
Урок Девять

1. открыт
2. Банк сейчас открыт?
3. Нет, это не правда.
4. Я не русский.
5. американец
6. Я американец.
7. центр
8. церемония
9. ёлка
10. цыплёнок
11. жук
12. ёжик
13. живёте
14. Где вы живёте?
15. Я живу в Москве.
16. таракан
17. царапина
18. Мне нравится цирк.
19. на юг
20. Пойдём на юг.

Part One

goRussian

Lesson Nine

1. open (masculine)
2. Is the bank open now?
3. No, that's not true.
4. I'm not Russian. (masculine)
5. an American (masculine)
6. I'm American. (masculine)
7. center; downtown
8. ceremony
9. fir tree
10. chick
11. bug
12. hedgehog
13. [you] live
14. Where do you live?
15. I live in Moscow.
16. cockroach
17. scratch
18. I like circus.
19. [to] south
20. Let's go south.

Part One
Урок Десять

1. чаша
2. груша
3. заяц
4. собака
5. плохо
6. плохая
7. плохая собака!
8. флаг
9. флот
10. цифра
11. русский флаг
12. подъезд
13. сел / съел
14. съехать
15. Я съеду.
16. щи
17. щи / шить
18. щёлк / шёлк
19. лещ
20. въехать

Part One
Lesson Ten

1. cup, bowl
2. a pear
3. hare
4. dog
5. [it's] bad
6. bad (f. adjective)
7. Bad dog!
8. flag
9. fleet
10. number; figure
11. Russian flag
12. entrance (of the residential building)
13. sat down (masculine) / ate up (masculine)
14. to drive down; move out
15. I will drive down.
16. cabbage soup
17. cabbage soup / to sew
18. snap (noun) / silk
19. bream (fish)
20. to drive into / to drive up

Part One

goRussian

Урок Одиннадцать

1. **Где Иван?**
2. **Он не здесь.**
3. **Может быть, он там.**
4. **Он не в гостинице.**
5. **Гостиница «Интурист»**
6. **Ольга в гостинице.**
7. **Она там.**
8. **Вы знаете?**
9. **Ты знаешь?**
10. **Нет, я не знаю.**
11. **ещё**
12. **Я ещё не знаю.**
13. **Не знаю, где Иван.**
14. **на Тверской улице**
15. **Моховая улица**
16. **зубов**
17. **Сколько зубов у акулы?**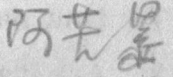
18. **Спросите у Ивана.**
19. **У меня заказан номер.**
20. **Чем он занимается?**

Part One

Lesson Eleven

1. Where's Ivan?
2. He's not here.
3. Maybe he's over there.
4. He's not in the hotel.
5. Hotel *Intourist*
6. Olga is in the hotel.
7. She's over there.
8. Do you know? (formal / plural)
9. Do you know? (informal)
10. No, I don't know.
11. still / yet
12. I don't know yet.
13. [I] don't know where Ivan is.
14. on Tverskaya Street
15. Mokhovaya Street
16. teeth (genitive case, plural)
17. How many teeth does a shark have?
18. Ask Ivan (genitive case).
19. I have a [hotel] room reserved.
20. What is he involved with? / What does he do?

Part One
Урок Двенадцать

1. Мы чихаем.
2. фабрика
3. ехать на автобусе
4. в аптеку
5. разъезд
6. пожалуйста
7. помочь
8. интернет кафе
9. Я люблю леща.
10. Борис, ты не прав.
11. Я раздражён.
12. Почему?
13. Хлеб подгорел.
14. Пётр Великий
15. зимой
16. наша дочь
17. Она приехала ---
18. Она приехала в Москву одна.
19. Мой сын тоже в Москве.
20. Вчера мы его видели.

Part One

*go*Russian

Lesson Twelve

1. We sneeze.
2. factory
3. to go by bus
4. to the pharmacy
5. journey, travels
6. please
7. to help
8. internet café
9. I like [love] bream.
10. Boris, you're not right.
11. I'm irritated.
12. Why?
13. The bread got burnt.
14. Peter the Great
15. in the winter
16. Our daughter
17. She came / arrived ---
18. She came to / arrived in Moscow alone.
19. My son is also in Moscow.
20. Yesterday we saw him.

Part One
Урок Тринадцать

1. капуста
2. играю
3. Очень хорошо.
4. «Аргументы и факты»
5. «Юный натуралист»
6. Мы читаем газету.
7. Это моя газета.
8. Я должен сказать Георгию.
9. Вымой своё лицо.
10. Наведите порядок.
11. Не курите, пожалуйста.
12. Нет дыма без огня.
13. кастрюля
14. У вас есть словарь?
15. Мы приехали вчера.
16. Мы ездили в музей.
17. Мы с сыном ---
18. Мы с сыном уже туда ездили.
19. У нас было мало времени.
20. Сегодня у меня много работы.

Part One   goRussian
Lesson Thirteen

1. cabbage
2. [I'm] playing
3. Very good.
4. *Arguments and Facts* (newspaper)
5. *Young Naturalist* (magazine)
6. We read / are reading newspaper.
7. This is my newspaper.
8. I have to (masculine) tell Georgiy.
9. Wash up your face.
10. Tidy up; sort out the mess; get [your house] in order
11. Don't smoke, please.
12. "There is no smoke without fire."
13. pan
14. Do you have a dictionary?
15. We arrived yesterday.
16. We went to the Museum.
17. My son and I ---
18. My son and I already went there.
19. We didn't have enough time.
20. Today I have a lot of work.

Part One
goRussian
Урок Четырнадцать

1. космонавт
2. Юрий Гагарин — космонавт.
3. Он первый космонавт.
4. река
5. река Волга
6. Это большая река.
7. Чёрное море
8. Хочу рыбу к ужину.
9. Я не люблю её.
10. У вас есть компьютер?
11. фотография
12. пирожок
13. пироги
14. мороженое
15. шашлык
16. Я очень голоден!
17. Он мой коллега.
18. Да, я его знаю.
19. Иван Петров — мой коллега.
20. Он из Петербурга.

Part One

*go*Russian

Lesson Fourteen

1. astronaut
2. Yuri Gagarin [is] an astronaut.
3. He's the first astronaut.
4. river
5. The Volga
6. It's a big river.
7. The Black Sea
8. [I] want fish for dinner.
9. I don't like [love] it [Meaning: her fish].
10. Do you have a computer?
11. photography
12. pastry
13. pirogy (pastries with meat / vegetable / fruit)
14. ice cream
15. kebab
16. I'm very hungry! (masculine)
17. He's my colleague.
18. Yes, I know him.
19. Ivan Petrov [is] my colleague.
20. He's from Petersburg.

Part One

goRussian

Урок Пятнадцать

1. карикатура
2. дождь на реке
3. папоротник
4. чебуреки
5. Это грузинское блюдо.
6. Как пройти в метро?
7. Идите прямо, а потом направо.
8. галерея
9. Третьяковская
10. Где Третьяковская галерея?
11. Это мой друг Иосиф.
12. Он большой оригинал.
13. Как её зовут?
14. Она тоже из Петербурга?
15. Вы говорите быстро.
16. Медленнее, пожалуйста.
17. Я собираюсь домой.
18. Давайте пойдём в центр.
19. Я скоро пойду в банк.
20. У меня будет много дел.

Part One
Lesson Fifteen

1. caricature
2. rain on the river
3. fern
4. cheburek (deep fried flat pasties filled with meat)
5. This is a Georgian dish (food).
6. How do I get to the Metro [station]?
7. Go straight ahead, and then to the right.
8. gallery
9. Tretyakov (f. adjective)
10. Where's Tretyakov Gallery?
11. This is my friend, Joseph.
12. He's very eccentric.
13. What's her name?
14. Is she also from Petersburg?
15. You speak quickly.
16. Slower, please.
17. I'm going to go home.
18. Let's go downtown.
19. I will soon go to the bank.
20. I will have a lot to do.

Part One

goRussian

Урок Шестнадцать

1. Я заболел.
2. У меня болит голова.
3. свинка
4. ветрянка
5. температура
6. желтуха
7. врач
8. скорая помощь
9. лекарства
10. больница
11. лучше
12. Мне уже лучше.
13. Спасибо большое!
14. Мы с вами ---
15. Мы с вами можем поужинать вместе?
16. Вам нравится ресторан «Арбат»?
17. Хорошо. Тогда до вечера.
18. нет аспирина
19. Как дела?
20. Отлично!

Part One

goRussian

Lesson Sixteen

1. I feel sick. (masculine)
2. I have a headache.
3. mumps
4. chicken pox
5. temperature
6. jaundice
7. doctor
8. ambulance
9. medicine (plural)
10. hospital
11. better
12. I'm better already.
13. Thank you very much!
14. You and I ---
15. Can you and I have dinner together?
16. Do you like the restaurant *Arbat*?
17. Good. Then see you in the evening. [Literally: until the evening.]
18. no aspirin
19. How are you? / How are things?
20. Excellent!

*go*Russian

Speak & Read the Pimsleur Way

· Reading Program ·

PART TWO

Part Two

*go*Russian

TABLE OF CONTENTS

Readings

Lesson One (Урок Один)	67
Lesson Two (Урок Два)	69
Lesson Three (Урок Три)	71
Lesson Four (Урок Четыре)	73
Lesson Five (Урок Пять)...................	75
Lesson Six (Урок Шесть)..................	77
Lesson Seven (Урок Семь)................	79
Lesson Eight (Урок Восемь)	81
Lesson Nine (Урок Девять)...............	83
Lesson Ten (Урок Десять).................	85
Lesson Eleven (Урок Одиннадцать).......	87
Lesson Twelve (Урок Двенадцать)	89
Lesson Thirteen (Урок Тринадцать)	91
Lesson Fourteen (Урок Четырнадцать)	93

Part Two

Урок Один

1. салат
2. самая красивая
3. Моя мама самая красивая.
4. где
5. Где она живёт?
6. Её семья жила в Туле.
7. в Москве
8. Я тоже жил там.
9. работы
10. каждый день
11. хоккей
12. самый
13. Я ехал домой на метро.
14. крокодил
15. Иногда я ходил пешком.
16. ваш брат

Part Two

Lesson One

1. salad
2. most beautiful (feminine)
3. My mother [is] the most beautiful.
4. where
5. Where does she live?
6. Her family lived in Tula.
7. in Moscow
8. I also lived (masculine) there.
9. work; jobs (plural, noun)
10. every day
11. hockey
12. the most (masculine)
13. I was going (masculine) home on the subway.
14. crocodile
15. Sometimes I went (masculine) for a walk.
16. your brother

Part Two
Урок Два

1. тёмная ночь
2. Чем бы
3. дитя
4. ни тешилось
5. ищу
6. шарманщик
7. Шарманщик играл на шарманке.
8. южный
9. Я работаю.
10. Не зевай!
11. рублей
12. казак
13. атаман
14. атаманом будешь
15. Терпи, казак, атаманом будешь!
16. цапля
17. в центр
18. подъём
19. Я живу в подъезде номер пять.
20. филин

Part Two   goRussian
Lesson Two

1. dark night
2. However / whatever
3. a child / a baby
4. enjoys oneself in whatever way
5. [I am] looking for
6. hand organist
7. The hand organist played the hand organ.
8. southern
9. I work.
10. Don't yawn!
11. rubles (genitive case, plural)
12. Cossack (cavalry soldier)
13. Ataman (old Russian military rank - as 'Marshal')
14. (an) Ataman (you) will be
15. Have patience, Cossack, you will be an Ataman!
16. heron
17. to town
18. ascent
19. I live in entrance number five. (Residential building in Russia can have several, numbered entrances.)
20. eagle owl

Part Two
Урок Три

1. недель
2. несколько недель
3. Мы здесь уже несколько недель.
4. Я купил газету ---
5. и кофе ---
6. моей жене.
7. Я ездил в магазин.
8. Но я ещё ничего не купил ---
9. моей дочери.
10. с друзьями
11. она живёт
12. Она там живёт с друзьями.
13. Станция недалеко.
14. ваш коллега
15. Это ваш коллега там?
16. Кто это?
17. когда-нибудь
18. Вы когда-нибудь были ---?
19. в Вашингтоне
20. Вы когда-нибудь были в Вашингтоне?

Part Two

Lesson Three

1. weeks (genitive case, plural)
2. a few weeks
3. We've been here already a few weeks.
4. I bought (masculine) a newspaper ---
5. and coffee ---
6. for my wife.
7. I went (masculine) to the store.
8. But I have not yet bought anything ---
9. for my daughter.
10. with friends
11. she lives
12. She lives there with friends.
13. The station isn't far.
14. your colleague (masculine)
15. Is that your colleague (masculine) over there?
16. Who is this / that?
17. ever
18. Have you ever been ---?
19. in Washington
20. Have you ever been in Washington?

Part Two

goRussian

Урок Четыре

1. После этого ---
2. кое-что
3. Я хотел бы кое-что купить в магазине.
4. моему сыну
5. Я должен кое-что купить моему сыну.
6. езжу
7. Иногда я туда езжу на метро.
8. До которого часа?
9. пешком
10. Или на метро.
11. Или на такси.
12. Ты не знаешь.
13. делаешь
14. во вторник
15. в пятницу
16. Что ты делаешь в пятницу?
17. У тебя есть время?
18. У тебя есть часы?
19. Я должен купить сувенир ---
20. моему другу.

Part Two

Lesson Four

1. after this / that ---
2. something
3. I'd like to (masc.) buy something in the store.
4. for my son
5. I have to (masc.) buy something for my son.
6. [I] go (by transportaion)
7. Sometimes I go there by subway.
8. Until what time?
9. on foot
10. Or by subway.
11. Or by taxi.
12. You don't know.
13. [you] are doing
14. on Tuesday
15. on Friday
16. What are you doing on Friday?
17. Do you have time?
18. Do you have a watch?
19. I have to (masculine) buy a souvenir ---
20. for my friend.

Part Two

Урок Пять

1. Добрый день, Наташа.
2. Извините ---
3. что
4. долго
5. Извините, что я так долго не писал вам.
6. У меня очень много работы ---
7. и очень мало времени.
8. Это правда!
9. Не было ничего нового.
10. А сегодня ---
11. я читал газету ---
12. и узнал, что ---
13. Волга впадает ---
14. в Каспийское море.
15. представляете
16. Вы представляете?
17. Пишите, пожалуйста.
18. Сергей

Part Two

goRussian

Lesson Five

1. Good day, Natasha.
2. I'm sorry ---
3. that
4. a long time
5. I'm sorry that I haven't written (masculine) you for a long time.
6. I have a lot of work ---
7. and very little time.
8. That's true!
9. There was nothing new.
10. But today ---
11. I was reading (masculine) the newspaper ---
12. and learned (masculine) that ---
13. the Volga runs ---
14. into the Caspian Sea.
15. imagine
16. (Can) you imagine?
17. Write, please.
18. Sergei

Part Two
goRussian
Урок Шесть

1. таможня
2. таможенная декларация
3. багаж и ручная кладь
4. два чемодана и сумка
5. иностранная валюта
6. США
7. доллары США и евро
8. золото и серебро
9. предметы
10. предметы старины
11. оружие и наркотики
12. откройте
13. Откройте этот чемодан.
14. Покажите вашу сумку.
15. Я везу подарки ---
16. моим друзьям.
17. У вас очень много подарков!
18. Нет, у меня много друзей.
19. Мне надо платить пошлину?
20. Нет, всё в порядке.

Part Two

goRussian

Lesson Six

1. customs
2. customs declaration
3. luggage (checked-in) and carry-on baggage
4. two suitcases and a bag
5. foreign currency
6. U.S.A.
7. U.S. dollars and euros
8. gold and silver
9. pieces
10. antiques ("old pieces")
11. drugs and narcotics
12. open
13. Open this suitcase.
14. Show me your bag.
15. I'm bringing gifts ---
16. for my friends.
17. You have a lot of gifts!
18. No, I have a lot of friends.
19. Do I need to pay a duty?
20. No, everything is in order.

Part Two
goRussian
Урок Семь

1. билет на самолёт
2. Где можно купить билет?
3. авиакасса
4. Авиакасса есть в гостинице «Метрополь».
5. лететь
6. Куда вы хотите лететь?
7. вылететь
8. Когда вы хотите вылететь?
9. Я хотел бы вылететь в четверг.
10. Мне нужен один билет.
11. «Аэрофлот»
12. компания «Аэрофлот»
13. Летайте самолётами «Аэрофлота»!
14. Нет, спасибо.
15. Может быть, в другой раз.
16. Аэропорт «Шереметьево»
17. задерживается
18. Ваш вылет ---
19. Ваш вылет задерживается.
20. Лучше поздно, чем никогда!

Part Two   goRussian
Lesson Seven

1. airline ticket [Literally: ticket for airplane]
2. Where is it possible to buy a ticket?
3. ticket office
4. There is a ticket office in the Hotel *Metropol*.
5. to fly
6. Where do you want to fly [to be flying]?
7. to fly away ("to leave by flying")
8. When do you want to fly (away)?
9. I'd like to (masculine) fly away on Thursday.
10. I need one ticket.
11. *Aeroflot*
12. *the Aeroflot* company
13. Fly *Aeroflot!* (Lit. Fly the planes of *Aeroflot!*)
14. No, thank you.
15. Maybe, another time.
16. *Sheremetyevo* Airport
17. be delayed
18. Your flight [Literally: take off] ---
19. Your flight has been delayed.
20. Better late than never!

Part Two

goRussian

Урок Восемь

1. метро
2. Московское метро
3. станция метро Пушкинская
4. Кольцевая линия
5. Осторожно!
6. Осторожно, двери закрываются.
7. Следующая станция — Маяковская.
8. Не прислоняться!
9. станция Проспект Мира
10. переход на Кольцевую линию
11. Поезд следует ---
12. Медведково
13. до станции Медведково.
14. Как доехать до гостиницы «Россия»?
15. выйти
16. Вам надо выйти на станции Китай-город.
17. Вам нужен жетон?
18. поздно
19. проездной
20. Спасибо, у меня есть проездной билет.

Part Two
Lesson Eight

1. subway
2. Moscow subway
3. Pushkinskaya subway station
4. Koltsevaya Line
5. Attention!
6. Attention, the doors are closing.
7. Next station --- Mayakovskaya.
8. Don't lean!
9. Prospekt Mira Station
10. transfer to the Kolstsevaya Line
11. (The) train goes ---
12. Medvedkovo
13. up to the Medvedkovo station.
14. How does one get to the Hotel *Russia*?
15. to get off
16. You need to get off at the Chinatown station.
17. Do you need a token?
18. late
19. pass
20. Thank you, I have a pass.

Part Two

Урок Девять

1. музеи и выставки
2. Московский Кремль
3. Вы хотите пойти в Кремль?
4. Мы уже были там вчера.
5. Мы ходили ---
6. в Оружейную Палату ---
7. в Алмазный Фонд ---
8. и в Покровский собор.
9. сегодня
10. Сегодня мы хотели бы попасть ---
11. в Третьяковскую галерею.
12. Туда можно поехать на метро.
13. Надо доехать до станции Третьяковская ---
14. и немного пройти пешком.
15. Мне очень нравятся ---
16. русские иконы.

Part Two

Lesson Nine

1. museums and exhibitions
2. Moscow Kremlin
3. Do you want to go to the Kremlin?
4. We were already there yesterday.
5. We went ---
6. to the Armory Chamber ---
7. to the Diamond Treasury ---
8. and to the Pokrovsky Cathedral.
9. today
10. Today we would like to get in ---
11. to the Tretyakov Gallery.
12. It's possible to go there by subway.
13. It's necessary to get to the Tretyakov Station ---
14. and (then) go a little further on foot.
15. I really like ---
16. Russian icons.

Part Two

Урок Десять

1. зоопарк
2. Московский зоопарк
3. Большая Грузинская улица
4. звери и птицы
5. Лев — царь зверей.
6. Кормить зверей —
7. воспрещается.
8. Курица — не птица.
9. Жираф большой —
10. ему видней.
11. страус
12. Страус прячет —
13. голову в песок.
14. Отойдите от клетки!
15. слон
16. Слону дали морковку.
17. Мой сын —
18. сейчас счастливый.

Part Two

goRussian

Lesson Ten

1. zoo
2. Moscow Zoo
3. Big Georgian Street
4. animals and birds
5. Lion - the tsar of the animals.
6. Feeding the animals ---
7. is forbidden.
8. A chicken is not a bird.
9. The giraffe is tall (Literally: big) ---
10. to him more is visible.
11. ostrich
12. The ostrich hides ---
13. his head in the sand.
14. Step away from the cage!
15. elephant
16. A carrot was given to the elephant.
17. My son ---
18. is happy now.

Part Two

Урок Одиннадцать

1. вход
2. выход
3. Нет выхода.
4. Курить воспрещается.
5. проезд
6. Сколько стоит проезд в метро?
7. Вам надо купить жетон.
8. Жетон стоит пять рублей.
9. На такси можно доехать быстрее.
10. Да, но такси намного дороже!
11. Тише едешь — дальше будешь.
12. остановка
13. остановка автобуса
14. трамвай
15. остановка трамвая
16. Нам лучше поехать на трамвае.
17. Нам надо проехать ---
18. Нам надо проехать три остановки.

Part Two

goRussian

Lesson Eleven

1. entrance
2. exit
3. No exit.
4. Smoking is forbidden.
5. ride
6. How much does a subway ride cost?
7. You need to buy a token.
8. The token costs five rubles.
9. By taxi it's possible to get where you're going more quickly.
10. Yes, but a taxi is much more expensive!
11. The more carefully you go, the further you get.
12. stop (for transportation)
13. bus stop
14. streetcar
15. streetcar stop
16. It's better for us to go by streetcar.
17. We need to go [Literally: pass] ---
18. We need to go three stops.

Part Two   *go***Russian**

Урок Двенадцать

1. Большой театр
2. в Большой театр
3. Вы хотите попасть в Большой театр?
4. А можно в Малый театр?
5. Что идёт сегодня?
6. спектакль
7. спектакль «Гроза»
8. А в Большом ---
9. Лебединое
10. балет «Лебединое озеро»
11. Куда вы хотите пойти?
12. Лучше в Большой.
13. Чайковского
14. Мне очень нравится музыка Чайковского.
15. Мы сможем достать билеты?
16. Давайте попробуем.

Part Two

*go*Russian

Lesson Twelve

1. Bolshoi Theater
2. to the Bolshoi Theater
3. Do you want to get in to the Bolshoi Theater?
4. But is it possible (to get into) the Maliy Theater?
5. What's playing today?
6. play
7. play *Thunderstorm*
8. And in the Bolshoi ---
9. (of a) Swan
10. The ballet *Swan Lake*
11. Where do you want to go?
12. It's better (to go) to the Bolshoi.
13. Tchaikovsky's
14. I like Tchaikovsky's music very much.
15. Will we be able to get tickets?
16. Let's try.

Part Two
Урок Тринадцать

1. Магазин «Книги»
2. «Книжный мир»
3. роман «Война и мир»
4. «Братья Карамазовы»
5. Мне очень нравится Пушкин.
6. У вас есть его книги?
7. «Руслан и Людмила»
8. роман «Евгений Онегин»
9. А что ещё у вас есть?
10. новое издание
11. новое издание Михаила Булгакова
12. «Мастер и Маргарита»
13. «Собачье сердце»
14. лучше
15. лучший
16. Книга — лучший подарок!

Part Two

goRussian

Lesson Thirteen

1. (the) store *Books*
2. *World of Books*
3. (the) novel *War and Peace*
4. *The Brothers Karamazov*
5. I like Pushkin very much.
6. Do you have his books?
7. *Ruslan and Ludmila*
8. (the) novel *Yevgeny Onegin*
9. And what else do you have?
10. new edition
11. a new edition of Mikhail Bulgakov
12. *The Master and Margarita*
13. *Heart of a Dog*
14. better
15. best
16. A book [is] the best gift!

Part Two   *goRussian*
Урок Четырнадцать

1. уезжаете
2. Вы уже уезжаете?
3. Да, мне уже пора домой.
4. В каком номере ---
5. В каком номере вы у нас жили?
6. Номер триста тридцать третий.
7. понравилось
8. Вам понравилось у нас?
9. Да, спасибо.
10. гостеприимный
11. Так, ваш номер стоит ---
12. Двести восемьдесят долларов в день.
13. Вы принимаете ---
14. кредитные карточки?
15. Да, конечно.
16. Пожалуйста, вот ваше такси.

Part Two   *go*Russian
Lesson Fourteen

1. are leaving
2. Are you already leaving?
3. Yes, it's already time (to go) home.
4. In which room (number) ---
5. In which room did you stay with us?
6. Number three hundred and thirty-three.
7. (you) enjoyed yourself
8. Did you enjoy yourself at our place?
9. Yes, thank you.
10. hospitable
11. So, your room costs ---
12. Two hundred eighty dollars per day.
13. Do you accept ---
14. credit cards?
15. Yes, of course.
16. Please, here's your taxi.

*go*Russian

Speak & Read the Pimsleur Way

· Reading Program ·

PART THREE

Part Three

goRussian

TABLE OF CONTENTS

Readings

Lesson One - (Урок Один) 99
Lesson Two - (Урок Два).................... 101
Lesson Three - (Урок Три) 103
Lesson Four - (Урок Четыре)................ 105
Lesson Five - (Урок Пять)................... 107
Lesson Six - (Урок Шесть) 109
Lesson Seven - (Урок Семь) 111
Lesson Eight - (Урок Восемь) 113
Lesson Nine - (Урок Девять) 115
Lesson Ten - (Урок Десять) 117
Lesson Eleven - (Урок Одиннадцать) 119
Lesson Twelve - (Урок Двенадцать)......... 121
Lesson Thirteen - (Урок Тринадцать)....... 123
Lesson Fourteen - (Урок Четырнадцать).... 125
Lesson Fifteen - (Урок Пятнадцать) 127
Lesson Sixteen - (Урок Шестнадцать) 129
Lesson Seventeen - (Урок Семнадцать)..... 131
Lesson Eighteen - (Урок Восемнадцать).... 133
Lesson Nineteen - (Урок Девятнадцать).... 135
Lesson Twenty - (Урок Двадцать).......... 137

Part Three

goRussian

Урок Один

1. Маша
2. мала
3. была
4. Маша была мала.
5. Маша ела кашу.
6. с маслом
7. Каша была с маслом.
8. с маслом и с молоком
9. Машу
10. мыла
11. Мама мыла Машу.
12. Мама мыла Машу с мылом.
13. нас
14. не домыла
15. Мама Машу не домыла.
16. Мыла было мало.
17. Мама купила ---
18. ещё мыла.
19. Мыло было дорогое.
20. Маша была красивая.

Part Three

Lesson One

1. Masha (f. name)
2. little, small (feminine)
3. was (feminine)
4. Masha was little.
5. Masha was eating oatmeal.
6. with butter
7. The oatmeal was with butter.
8. with butter and with milk
9. Masha (accusative case)
10. was washing (feminine)
11. Mama was washing Masha.
12. Mama was washing Masha with soap.
13. us
14. did not finish washing
15. Mama did not finish washing Masha.
16. There wasn't enough soap. [Literally: The soap was not enough.]
17. Mama bought ---
18. more soap.
19. The soap was expensive.
20. Masha was beautiful.

Part Three
Урок Два

1. заказ
2. Вас
3. Как Вас зовут?
4. Вас зовут Саша?
5. прошу
6. лошадка
7. плот
8. улица
9. подъезд
10. первый подъезд
11. двадцать
12. дом двадцать
13. двадцать шесть
14. квартира двадцать шесть
15. большая квартира
16. красивая квартира
17. красивый
18. Это красивый дом!
19. Это эскалатор.
20. Это замок.

Part Three
Lesson Two

1. an order
2. you (accusative / genetive case)
3. What's your name?
4. Is your name Sasha?
5. [I am] asking
6. a small horse
7. a raft
8. street
9. entrance
10. first entrance
11. twenty
12. building twenty
13. twenty-six
14. apartment twenty-six
15. big apartment
16. beautiful apartment
17. beautiful (masculine)
18. This is a beautiful building!
19. This is an escalator.
20. This is a lock.

Part Three
Урок Три

1. Вы забыли.
2. Простите.
3. Привет!
4. сможем
5. у мужа и жены
6. Извините ---
7. хороший
8. Ваш знакомый
9. площадь
10. Прошу прощения.
11. Где?
12. живёт
13. Где живёт Ваш знакомый?
14. Я не знаю.
15. Простите, я забыл.
16. Борис
17. Что?
18. Что ещё?
19. Что ещё Вы не знаете?
20. Я не знаю, где Вы живёте.

Part Three

*go*Russian

Lesson Three

1. You forgot.
2. Forgive me.
3. Hi!
4. [We] will be able to
5. the husband and wife have
6. Excuse me ---
7. good (adj., m.)
8. your aquaintance
9. city square
10. I beg your pardon.
11. Where?
12. lives
13. Where does your aquaintance live?
14. I don't know.
15. Forgive me, I forgot. (masculine)
16. Boris
17. What?
18. What else?
19. What else don't you know?
20. I don't know where you live.

Part Three
Урок Четыре

1. уважаемые
2. Уважаемые пассажиры!
3. Федерации
4. Российской Федерации
5. Наш самолёт произвёл посадку ---
6. в столице Российской Федерации.
7. международный
8. Международный аэропорт ---
9. «Шереметьево Два»
10. Добро пожаловать в Москву!
11. Сейчас шесть часов утра ---
12. и в Москве идёт снег.
13. пограничный контроль
14. Ваши документы, пожалуйста.
15. Вот мой паспорт.
16. Я получил визу ---
17. в Нью-Йорке.
18. в консульстве России
19. Да, всё в порядке.
20. Где я могу получить свой багаж?

Part Three
goRussian
Lesson Four

1. respected
2. Respected passengers!
3. (of the) federation
4. (of the) Russian Federation
5. Our plane has landed ---
6. in the capital of the Russian Federation.
7. international
8. International Airport ---
9. *Sheremetyevo 2*
10. Welcome to Moscow!
11. It's now six o'clock in the morning ---
12. and it's snowing in Moscow.
13. border control
14. Your documents, please.
15. Here is my passport.
16. I received (masculine) a visa ---
17. in New York.
18. in the Russian consulate
19. Yes, everything is in order.
20. Where I can pick up my luggage?

Part Three

goRussian

Урок Пять

1. доехать
2. до гостиницы
3. Как доехать до гостиницы «Нева»?
4. на автобусе
5. Туда можно доехать на автобусе.
6. вначале
7. Вначале на автобусе, а потом на метро.
8. Или, может быть, на такси.
9. невозможно
10. Туда невозможно ехать на машине.
11. На такси – быстрее.
12. дешевле
13. На автобусе – дешевле.
14. Сколько стоит такси?
15. лучше
16. Лучше не спрашивайте!
17. Вы туда поедете на такси?
18. друзья
19. Меня должны встретить мои друзья.
20. К сожалению, их нет.

Part Three

goRussian

Lesson Five

1. to get to
2. to the hotel
3. How does one get to the Hotel *Neva*?
4. by bus
5. You can get there by bus.
6. at first
7. At first by bus, and then by subway.
8. Or, maybe, by taxi.
9. impossible
10. It's impossible to go there by car.
11. By taxi is faster.
12. cheaper
13. By bus is cheaper.
14. How much does a taxi cost?
15. better
16. Better not to ask!
17. Will you go there by taxi?
18. friends
19. My friends are supposed to meet me.
20. Unfortunately, they're not here.

Part Three

Урок Шесть

goRussian

1. водительские права
2. дорожного
3. правила дорожного движения
4. «Лада»
5. У Вас «Волга» или «Москвич»?
6. Нет, у меня «Лада».
7. сигналы
8. сигналы светофора
9. зелёный свет
10. запрещён
11. Поворот налево запрещён.
12. Проезд закрыт.
13. ремонт дороги
14. Обгон запрещён.
15. перекрёсток
16. Водитель чёрной «Волги» ---
17. остановите машину!
18. Кажется, мы приехали.
19. автоинспектор
20. Это автоинспектор.

Part Three

goRussian

Lesson Six

1. driver's license
2. (of the) road
3. road regulations or traffic rules
4. *Lada* (make of a Russian car)
5. Do you have a *Volga* or a *Moskvich*?
6. No, I have a *Lada*.
7. signals
8. traffic light signals
9. green light
10. forbidden
11. Turning to the left is forbidden.
12. The way is closed.
13. road work
14. No passing. ("Passing is forbidden.")
15. intersection
16. Driver of the black *Volga* ---
17. stop the car!
18. It seems that we have arrived.
19. road police officer
20. It's a road police officer.

Part Three   **goRussian**

Урок Семь

1. Ресторан «Славянский базар»
2. Что сегодня есть в меню?
3. закуски
4. чёрная икра
5. первые блюда
6. борщ по-флотски
7. котлеты
8. котлеты по-киевски
9. Что Вы будете пить?
10. Московскую водку?
11. армянский
12. Московскую водку или армянский коньяк?
13. Балтику номер шесть
14. Мы хотели бы заказать бутылку вина.
15. А на десерт?
16. мороженое
17. мороженое и кисель
18. счёт
19. Принесите счёт, пожалуйста.
20. Всё было очень вкусно.

Part Three
Lesson Seven

1. the restaurant *Slaviansky Bazar*
2. What is on the menu today?
3. appetizers
4. black caviar
5. first courses
6. borshch Navy-style
7. cutlets
8. chicken Kiev ("cutlets Kiev-syle")
9. What you will drink?
10. Moscow vodka?
11. Armenian
12. Moscow vodka or Armenian cognac?
13. Baltika Number Six (a Russian beer)
14. We'd like to order a bottle of wine.
15. And for desert?
16. ice-cream
17. ice-cream and kisel (Russian dessert)
18. bill / check
19. Bring the check, please.
20. Everything was very delicious.

Part Three
Урок Восемь

1. Тверская улица
2. подземный переход
3. Красная площадь
4. Страстной бульвар
5. театр имени Маяковского
6. иностранной
7. Библиотека иностранной литературы
8. Посторонним вход воспрещён!
9. Манежная площадь
10. центральный
11. выставочный
12. Центральный выставочный зал
13. государственный
14. Московский государственный университет
15. МГУ
16. Выход к Курскому вокзалу
17. Места для пассажиров с детьми
18. предварительной
19. Касса предварительной ---
20. продажи билетов

Part Three

Lesson Eight

1. Tverskaya Street
2. underground crosswalk
3. Red Square
4. Strastnoi Boulevard
5. Maiakovsky Theater
6. (of) foreign
7. Library of Foreign Literature
8. No trespassing.
9. Manezhnaya Square
10. central
11. exhibition
12. Central Exhibition Hall
13. state
14. Moscow State University
15. M.G.U.
16. Exit to the Kurski train station
17. Places for passengers with children
18. preliminary
19. Office for the preliminary (pre-sale) ---
20. sale of tickets

Part Three
*go*Russian
Урок Девять

1. кассы
2. Билетные кассы
3. Два билета до Самары, пожалуйста.
4. На двадцать пятое мая.
5. плацкартный
6. В плацкартный вагон?
7. Нет, лучше в купейный.
8. купейный / купейных
9. К сожалению, купейных мест нет.
10. Есть два места в мягком вагоне.
11. Хорошо, я возьму ---
12. Я возьму эти билеты.
13. Пятый вагон, места три и четыре.
14. Поезд номер семнадцать.
15. Во сколько?
16. Отправление из Москвы ---
17. с Казанского вокзала ---
18. в девятнадцать часов.
19. Прибытие в Самару ---
20. в одиннадцать сорок пять.

Part Three

*go*Russian

Lesson Nine

1. (booking / box) offices
2. Ticket offices
3. Two tickets to Samara, please.
4. On the twenty-fifth of May.
5. reserved seating
6. In the reserved seating car (wagon)?
7. No, better in the compartment (car).
8. compartment / (of a) compartment
9. Unfortunately, the compartment (car) has no (available) places.
10. There are two places in the sleeping car.
11. OK, I'll take ---
12. I'll take those tickets.
13. The fifth car, seats three and four.
14. Train number seventeen.
15. At what time?
16. Departure from Moscow ---
17. from the Kazan train station ---
18. at nineteen o'clock. (7 P.M.)
19. Arrival in Samara ---
20. at eleven forty-five.

Part Three
goRussian

Урок Десять

1. Где стоит Ваша машина?
2. припарковались
3. Скажите, где Вы припарковались?
4. Я припарковался на улице ---
5. На улице рядом с домом.
6. Нам надо поговорить ---
7. о наших планах.
8. У нас скоро будет ---
9. важная встреча.
10. подготовить
11. Я должен подготовить её.
12. переводчик
13. Там будет переводчик?
14. Мне кажется, что ---
15. он сейчас в Германии.
16. в Германии / в Москве
17. Его не будет в Москве ---
18. на этой неделе.
19. Он приезжает в Москву ---
20. в следующем году.

Part Three
goRussian

Lesson Ten

1. Where is your car parked?
2. (you) parked
3. Tell me, where did you park?
4. I parked (masculine) on the street ---
5. On the street next to the building.
6. We need to talk ---
7. about our plans.
8. We will soon have ---
9. an important meeting.
10. to get ready / to prepare
11. I'm supposed (masculine) to get it ready.
12. interpreter
13. Will an interpreter be there?
14. It seems to me, that ---
15. he is now in Germany.
16. in Germany / in Moscow
17. He won't be in Moscow ---
18. this week.
19. He's coming to Moscow ---
20. next year.

Part Three

goRussian

Урок Одиннадцать

1. Здравствуйте, Иван Сергеевич!
2. Как прошла Ваша поездка в Америку?
3. Прекрасно, спасибо.
4. А что Вы делаете?
5. Чем Вы занимаетесь?
6. Чем Вы любите заниматься?
7. В свободное время ---
8. **Я** занимаюсь ---
9. **Я** занимаюсь спортом.
10. **Я** люблю ---
11. **Я** очень люблю ---
12. в шахматы
13. **Я** очень люблю играть в шахматы.
14. Но мне надо узнать, ---
15. как прошёл проект.
16. Вы не можете ---
17. посмотреть
18. Вы не можете мне показать документы?
19. Мне говорили ---
20. Мне говорили, что проект уже закончен.

Part Three

goRussian

Lesson Eleven

1. Hello, Ivan Sergeevich!
2. How did your trip to America go?
3. Beautifully, thanks.
4. And what are you doing?
5. What do you do? / What are you doing? [formal]
6. What is your hobby?
7. In (my) free time ---
8. I occupy myself with ---
9. I play sports.
10. I like [love] (to) ---
11. I very much like to ---
12. (at) chess
13. I very much like to play chess.
14. But I need to find out ---
15. how the project went.
16. You can't ---
17. to have a look / take a look
18. Can you [Lit. you can't] show me the documents?
19. I was told ---
20. I was told that the project is already finished.

Part Three
Урок Двенадцать

1. Вы могли ---
2. прийти
3. Не могли бы Вы ---?
4. Не могли бы Вы прийти в три?
5. Не раньше, и не позже.
6. Это невозможно.
7. Вам не надо перезвонить ---
8. но, пожалуйста ---
9. подождите ---
10. потому, что я не знаю ---
11. как лучше пройти ---
12. к Вам домой.
13. У нас новый адрес.
14. Алтуфьевское
15. Конечно, мне его трудно найти.
16. Вы знаете, что у меня здесь ---
17. нет машины.
18. Машина не нужна.
19. Где здесь такси?
20. Туда лучше ездить на метро.

Part Three

goRussian

Lesson Twelve

1. You were able to ---
2. to arrive (on foot, in general)
3. Could you ---? [Literally: Couldn't you ---?]
4. Could you [Lit. Couldn't you] arrive at three?
5. Not earlier, and not later.
6. That's impossible.
7. You don't need to call back ---
8. but please ---
9. wait ---
10. because I don't know ---
11. the best way to get to ---
12. (to) your house.
13. We have a new address.
14. Altufievskoe (name of an avenue)
15. Of course, it's difficult for me to find it.
16. You know, that I have here ---
17. no car.
18. A car isn't necessary.
19. Where is there a taxi here?
20. It's better to take the subway there.

Part Three **goRussian**

Урок Тринадцать

1. Извините ---
2. Вы не знаете ---
3. Извините, Вы не знаете, откуда я могу позвонить?
4. Не отсюда.
5. Я скоро должен позвонить.
6. Я работаю в Москве уже семь лет.
7. через три года
8. три месяца
9. Через три дня ---
10. у меня будет новая работа.
11. Я нашёл ---
12. новую работу.
13. Президент компании сейчас в Петербурге.
14. У него там очень важная встреча ---
15. с нашим новым клиентом.
16. Он будет работать в Петербурге?
17. Его не будет в Москве ---
18. до пятницы.
19. И, тогда, до этого ---
20. у меня будет свободное время.

Part Three

goRussian

Lesson Thirteen

1. Excuse me ---
2. Do you know --- (formal) [Lit. You don't know.]
3. Excuse me, do you know [from] where I can make a call here?
4. Not from here.
5. I'm soon supposed to (masculine) make a call
6. I've been working in Moscow already seven years.
7. in three years
8. three months
9. In three days ---
10. I will have a new job.
11. I found --- (masculine)
12. a new job.
13. The president of the company is now in Petersburg.
14. He has a very important meeting there ---
15. with our new client.
16. He'll be working in Petersburg?
17. He won't be in Moscow ---
18. until Friday.
19. And, therefore, until then ---
20. I will have free time.

Part Three

goRussian

Урок Четырнадцать

1. У Вас заказан номер?
2. Да, у меня заказан номер на сегодня.
3. Сегодня праздник.
4. число
5. Какое сегодня число?
6. Который сейчас час?
7. Сейчас полпятого.
8. Мне уже пора ехать.
9. Куда Вы уезжаете?
10. Что Вы хотите?
11. Чем Вы любите ---?
12. Чем Вы любите заниматься?
13. Чем занимается Ваш сын?
14. Мой сын ищет работу.
15. Кем он работает?
16. Он сейчас работает инженером.
17. Какую работу он ищет?
18. Кем он хочет стать?
19. Он хочет стать учителем.
20. Он хочет преподавать историю.

Part Three

*go*Russian

Lesson Fourteen

1. Do you have a [hotel] room reserved?
2. Yes, I have a room reserved for today.
3. Today is a holiday.
4. date
5. What's today's date?
6. What time is it?
7. Now it's half past four.
8. It's already time for me to be going.
9. Where are you leaving for?
10. What do you want?
11. What do you like (to) ---?
12. What do you like to do ("to be involved in")?
13. What is your son doing?
14. My son is looking for a job.
15. What does he do?
16. He now works as an engineer.
17. What job is he looking for?
18. What does he want to become?
19. He wants to become a teacher.
20. He wants to teach history.

Part Three

*go*Russian

Урок Пятнадцать

1. Скажите, пожалуйста, Ваш муж здесь?
2. Когда он должен вернуться?
3. состояться
4. У нас с ним ---
5. должна была состояться встреча.
6. состоится
7. Когда состоится встреча?
8. Скоро начинается ---
9. сегодняшняя
10. Скоро начинается сегодняшняя встреча.
11. У Вас с собой ---
12. У Вас с собой есть документы?
13. Через час ---
14. приезжает президент ---
15. из Москвы.
16. Я хотел бы его подождать.
17. Я хотел бы ему показать документы.
18. Я их получил ---
19. из Америки ---
20. в прошлом году.

Part Three   goRussian
Lesson Fifteen

1. Tell me, please, is your husband here?
2. When is he supposed to return?
3. to take place
4. He and I ---
5. were supposed to have a meeting.
6. will take place / is going to taking place
7. When is the meeting going to take place?
8. Soon begins ---
9. today's
10. Today's meeting begins soon.
11. Do you have with you ---?
12. Do you have the documents with you?
13. In an hour ---
14. the president is arriving ---
15. from Moscow.
16. I'd like (masculine) to wait for him.
17. I'd like to (masc.) show him the documents.
18. I received (masculine) them ---
19. from America ---
20. last year.

Part Three

goRussian

Урок Шестнадцать

1. У тебя красивая квартира!
2. Она очень большая.
3. Ты не знаешь ---
4. дойти
5. дойти до центра
6. Отсюда можно дойти до центра пешком?
7. Я думаю, что ---
8. на метро быстрее.
9. Почему ты хочешь идти пешком?
10. Тебе нравится ходить пешком?
11. погулять
12. пойти погулять
13. Я ищу ---
14. Я ищу квартиру ---
15. моего коллеги.
16. Я не могу найти его адрес.
17. У Вас есть карта города?
18. Да, конечно, есть ---
19. но Вам было бы лучше ---
20. поехать на метро.

Part Three

goRussian

Lesson Sixteen

1. You have a beautiful apartment!
2. It's very big.
3. Do you know --- (informal) [Lit. You don't know.]
4. to get to
5. to get downtown
6. From here, is it possible to get downtown on foot?
7. I think that ---
8. by the subway is faster.
9. Why do you want to go on foot?
10. Do you like to travel on foot?
11. take a walk
12. to go for a walk
13. I'm looking for ---
14. I'm looking for the apartment ---
15. of my colleague.
16. I can't find his address.
17. Do you have a map of the city?
18. Yes, of course, I do, ---
19. but it would be better for you ---
20. to take the subway.

Part Three
goRussian
Урок Семнадцать

1. У Вас есть кредитная карточка?
2. кредитные карточки
3. Вы принимаете кредитные карточки?
4. Нет, к сожалению.
5. У меня мало денег.
6. У Вас нет русских денег?
7. копейка
8. У меня только кредитная карточка.
9. свободного
10. У Вас нет свободного времени?
11. Вчера пришёл мой друг.
12. Как его зовут?
13. Как зовут Вашего друга?
14. Николаевич
15. Его зовут Борис Николаевич.
16. телефонная книга
17. Вы знаете его телефон?
18. Вы знаете код Москвы?
19. девяносто пять
20. Код Москвы ноль девяносто пять.

Part Three

goRussian

Lesson Seventeen

1. Do you have a credit card?
2. credit cards
3. Do you accept credit cards?
4. No, unfortunately.
5. I have little money.
6. You don't have any Russian money?
7. kopecks (coins)
8. I have only a credit card.
9. (of) free
10. You don't have any free time?
11. My friend came yesterday.
12. What is his name?
13. What is your friend's name?
14. Nikolaevich
15. His name is Boris Nikolaevich.
16. phone book
17. Do you know his telephone number?
18. Do you know the (area) code for Moscow?
19. ninety-five
20. The code for Moscow is zero ninety-five.

Part Three

*go*Russian

Урок Восемнадцать

1. На сколько?
2. Как долго ---?
3. длиться
4. конференция
5. Когда начинается конференция?
6. Как долго она будет длиться?
7. Она скоро начинается?
8. Как долго будет длиться конференция?
9. Вы должны подготовить её?
10. Кто должен ---?
11. Кто должен подготовить эту встречу?
12. Я забыла.
13. У меня должна состояться ---
14. У меня должна состояться встреча с президентом.
15. Мне надо туда прийти ---
16. вовремя.
17. Я должен подготовить конференцию.
18. Вы готовы?
19. Будь готов!
20. Всегда готов!

Part Three

goRussian

Lesson Eighteen

1. For how long?
2. How long ---?
3. to last
4. conference
5. When is the conference beginning?
6. How long will it last?
7. Is it beginning soon?
8. How long will the conference last?
9. Are you supposed to get it ready?
10. Who is supposed to ---?
11. Who is supposed to get this meeting ready?
12. I forgot. (feminine)
13. I'm supposed to have ---
14. I'm supposed to have a meeting with the president.
15. I need to arrive there ---
16. on time.
17. I'm supposed to (m) get the conference ready.
18. Are you ready?
19. Be ready!
20. Always ready!

Part Three

Урок Девятнадцать

1. Извините, Елена Сергеевна!
2. Вы не знаете, ---
3. сколько стоит билет в театр?
4. Я не знаю, ---
5. можете ли Вы мне помочь.
6. Да, конечно, могу.
7. А Вы не можете мне сказать ---
8. Как лучше отсюда пройти в кино?
9. Сегодня идёт новый фильм.
10. Но у меня сегодня ---
11. очень много работы.
12. кто-нибудь
13. Мне кто-нибудь звонил?
14. сообщение
15. Кто-нибудь оставил сообщение?
16. Вам звонил президент компании.
17. Мне звонил президент?
18. Да, но он не оставил сообщения.
19. сообщение / сообщения
20. После этого Вам никто не звонил.

Part Three

goRussian

Lesson Nineteen

1. Excuse me, Yelena Sergeevna!
2. Do you know --- (formal) [Lit. You don't know.]
3. how much a theater ticket costs?
4. I don't know ---
5. whether you can help me.
6. Yes, of course, [I] can.
7. And can you tell me --- [Lit. And you can't tell me]
8. What's the best way to get to the cinema from here?
9. Today a new movie is playing.
10. But I have, today, ---
11. a lot of work.
12. anyone
13. Did anyone call for me?
14. message
15. Did anyone leave a message?
16. The president of the company called you.
17. The president called me?
18. Yes, but he didn't leave a message.
19. message / messages
20. After that, no one called you.

Part Three
goRussian
Урок Двадцать

1. Сейчас мы готовы заказать.
2. две порции
3. Нам две порции котлет по-киевски, пожалуйста.
4. А что Вы будете пить?
5. бутылка
6. Нам бутылку красного вина.
7. свободного
8. У нас сейчас есть ---
9. У нас сейчас есть свободное время.
10. Тогда, не могли бы Вы ---
11. Не хотели бы Вы ---
12. Не хотели бы Вы пойти со мной ---
13. в парк?
14. поиграть
15. Не хотели бы Вы поиграть со мной ---
16. в шахматы?
17. Спасибо, но мне кажется ---
18. Мне кажется, что уже поздно.
19. Мы с мужем завтра ---
20. приезжаем к Вам в гости.

Part Three

*go*Russian

Lesson Twenty

1. Now we're ready to order.
2. two portions
3. For us, two portions of chicken Kiev, please.
4. And what will you be drinking?
5. bottle
6. A bottle of red wine for us.
7. (of) free
8. We now have ---
9. We now have free time.
10. Then could you [Literally: couldn't you] ---
11. Would [Literally: wouldn't] you like to ---
12. Would you like to go with me ---
13. to the park?
14. to play
15. Wouldn't you like to play with me ---
16. at chess?
17. Thank you, but it seems to me ---
18. It seems to me that it's already late.
19. My husband and I tomorrow ---
20. will come to visit you.

Pimsleur® Language Programs are available in all of the commonly spoken languages.

Programs in many other languages are also available. For more information, call 1-800-831-5497 or visit us at www.Pimsleur.com

Notes

PIMSLEUR'S RUSSIAN LANGUAGE PROGRAMS

• •

Russian Comprehensive, Level I

Learn to Speak and Understand Russian
Compact Disk
ISBN: 9780743506205

(16 CDs) 16 hours of instruction - thirty 30-minute lessons with Reading Lessons. Designed for those who want to gain fluency with 400-500 vocabulary words and several hundred sentence structures.

Notes

PIMSLEUR'S RUSSIAN LANGUAGE PROGRAMS

• •

Russian Comprehensive, Level II

Learn to Speak and Understand Russian
Compact Disk
ISBN: 9780743525985

(16 CDs) An additional 16 hours of instruction. Level II builds on Level I with 30 additional 30-minute lessons, plus Reading Lessons.

For those who wish to expand their vocabulary and increase fluency.

Notes

PIMSLEUR'S RUSSIAN LANGUAGE PROGRAMS

● ●

Russian Comprehensive, Level III

Learn to Speak and Understand Russian
Compact Disk
ISBN: 9780743528917

(16 CDs) An additional 16 hours of instruction. Builds on Levels I and II, with 30 additional 30-minute lessons, plus Reading Lessons.

For those who wish to expand their vocabulary and increase fluency to an even higher level.

Notes

PIMSLEUR'S OTHER SLAVIC LANGUAGE PROGRAMS

East Slavic language
- **Ukrainian**

West Slavic languages
- **Czech**
- **Polish**

South Slavic language
- **Croatian**

Notes

PIMSLEUR'S ENGLISH FOR RUSSIAN SPEAKERS LANGUAGE PROGRAMS

● ●

**English for Russian Speakers
Comprehensive Program, Level I**

Learn to Speak and Understand English as a Second Language
Compact Disk
ISBN: 9780671776558

Comprehensive English I includes 30 lessons of essential grammar and vocabulary -- 16 hours of real-life spoken practice sessions -- plus an introduction to reading.

Upon completion of this Level I program, you will have functional spoken proficiency with the most-frequently-used vocabulary and grammatical structures.

Notes

Чтобы получить дополнительную информацию, – позвоните по телефону 1-800-831-5497 или посетите наш сайт на Интернете: www.Pimsleur.com

Notes

Pimsleur programs are also available in the following languages:

- Albanian
- Arabic (Eastern)
- Arabic (Egyptian)
- Armenian (Eastern)
- Armenian (Western)
- Chinese (Cantonese)
- Chinese (Mandarin)
- Croatian
- Czech
- Danish
- Dari (Persian)
- Dutch
- Farsi (Persian)
- French
- German
- Greek
- Haitian Creole
- Hebrew
- Hindi
- Hungarian
- Indonesian
- Irish
- Italian
- Japanese
- Korean
- Lithuanian
- Norwegian
- Ojibwe
- Polish
- Portuguese (Brazilian)
- Portuguese (European)
- Romanian
- Russian
- Spanish *(for Children & Adults)*
- Swahili
- Swedish
- Swiss German
- Tagalog
- Thai
- Turkish
- Twi
- Ukrainian
- Urdu
- Vietnamese

English as a Second Language (ESL) programs are available for native-speakers of the following languages:

- Arabic
- Chinese (Cantonese)
- Chinese (Mandarin)
- Farsi (Persian)
- French
- German
- Haitian Creole
- Hindi
- Italian
- Korean
- Portuguese
- Russian
- Spanish
- Vietnamese